BoE 3956

HANS-GÜNTER HEUMANN

Children's Classic Piano

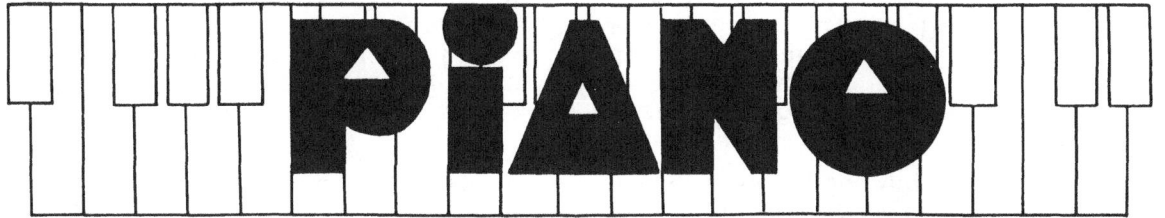

KUNTERBUNTE SPIELKISTE
BELIEBTER KLASSISCHER
MELODIEN IN LEICHTESTER
BIS LEICHTER FASSUNG
FÜR KLAVIER/KEYBOARD

A PLAYBOX ASSORTMENT OF
POPULAR CLASSICAL
MELODIES IN EASY AND
VERY EASY ARRANGEMENTS
FOR PIANO/KEYBOARD

Heft 1 - Book 1

© Copyright MCMLXXXVI by Bosworth & Co.

BOSWORTH EDITION

Vorwort

Dieses Spielheft bietet dem Klavieranfänger schon sehr früh die Möglichkeit, neben der Klavierschule bekannte und beliebte klassische Melodien zu spielen.

Da jedoch die meisten dieser Melodien in ihrer ursprünglichen Form entweder gar nicht für Klavier oder aber schwierig gesetzt sind, wird der beginnende Klavierspieler mit den sorgfältigen Bearbeitungen und den ebenfalls in diesem Heft enthaltenen ersten Originalstücken großer Meister seinen spieltechnischen Stand erweitern können.

Langjährige Unterrichtserfahrung hat gezeigt, daß gerade der Anfänger glücklich über jedes Erfolgserlebnis ist und sich motiviert schwierigeren Aufgaben zuwenden kann.

Die enthaltenen Bearbeitungen sind aus diesem Grund noch möglichst einfach und kindgerecht, aber dennoch differenziert und pädagogisch wertvoll gehalten.

Alle Spielstücke dieser kunterbunten Spielkiste beliebter klassischer Melodien sind progressiv geordnet.

Foreword

With this book, the piano beginner can become acquainted with the well-known works of the Classical repertoire as an adjunct to his or her normal learning material.

Most of these pieces were originally written either for instruments other than the piano or were for more advanced pianists, but in this collection the young pianist's technique will benefit from the careful arrangements and also from the inclusion of original piano pieces by the great composers.

Many years of teaching experience have demonstrated that the greater the sense of achievement in beginners, the greater is their motivation to devote themselves to more difficult work.

Thus, the object of the book is to provide the simplest possible arrangements suitable for children, at the same time maintaining their proper character and educational value.

The pieces in this "playbox assortment of popular classics" are assembled in progressive order of difficulty.

Hinweis für Keyboard-Spieler:

- Spiele die rechte Hand sämtlicher Stücke wie notiert.
- Die linke Hand spielt nach den angegebenen Akkordsymbolen oberhalb des Notensystems, entweder als *'fingered chords'* gegriffene Akkorde) oder als *'single-fingered chords'* - SFC - (Einfingerbegleitautomatik).

Attention Keyboarders!

- Play the right hand part throughout as written.
- If the left hand is playing from the chord symbols above the stave, either *'fingered chords'* or *'single fingered chords'* - SFC - will do.

INHALT/INDEX

	Seite/Page
Freude schöner Götterfunken/The Hymn to Joy (Ludwig van Beethoven)	4
Cancan aus "Orpheus in der Unterwelt" (Jacques Offenbach)	5
Champagner-Arie/Champagne Aria (Wolfgang Amadeus Mozart)	6
Brautchor/The Wedding March (Richard Wagner)	7
Militärmarsch/Military March (Franz Schubert)	8
Largo aus der 9. Symphonie (Anton Dvořák)	9
Kaiserwalzer/Emperor Waltz (Johann Strauß, Sohn)	10
Wiegenlied/Lullaby (Johannes Brahms)	12
Für Elise (Ludwig van Beethoven)	13
An der schönen blauen Donau/The Blue Danube (Johann Strauß, Sohn)	14
O wie so trügerisch/La donna è mobile (Giuseppe Verdi)	16
Menuett/Minuet (Jean-Philippe Rameau)	18
Deutscher Tanz/German Dance (Ludwig van Beethoven)	19
Sehnsuchtswalzer/Longing (Franz Schubert)	20
Menuett/Minuet (Wolfgang Amadeus Mozart)	21
Gefangenenchor/Captives' Chorus (Giuseppe Verdi)	22
Menuett/Minuet (Johann Sebastian Bach)	24
Plaisir d'amour (Jean Martini)	26
Marsch/March (Georges Bizet)	27
Eine kleine Nachtmusik (Wolfgang Amadeus Mozart)	28
Ungarischer Tanz/Hungarian Dance (Johannes Brahms)	30
Tristesse (Frédéric Chopin)	32
Liebestraum (Franz Liszt)	34
Ecossaise (Franz Schubert)	35
Rondo alla turca/Turkish March (Wolfgang Amadeus Mozart)	36
Mazurka (Hans-Günter Heumann)	38
Träumerei/Dreaming (Robert Schumann)	40

Freude schöner Götterfunken
The Hymn to Joy
aus der 9. Sinfonie

Ludwig van Beethoven (1770-1827)
Arr.: Hans-Günter Heumann

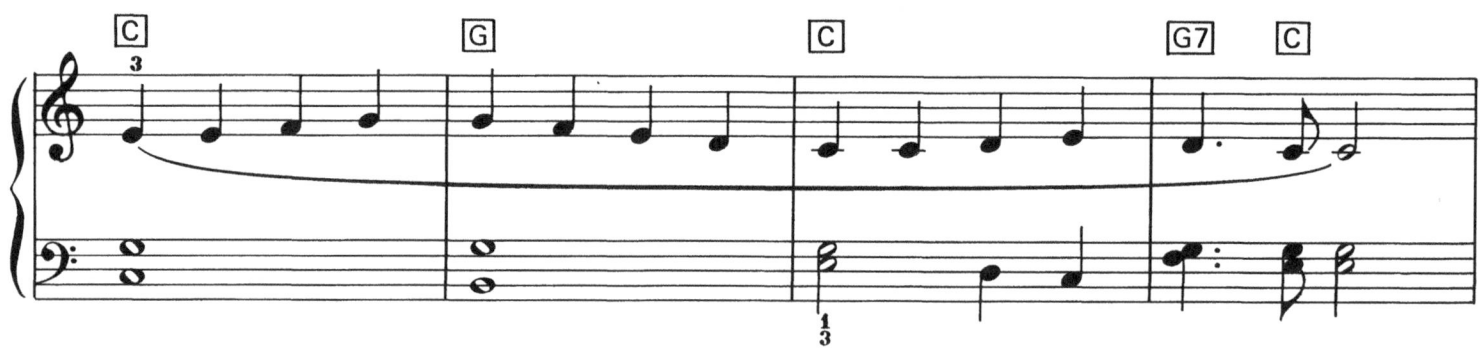

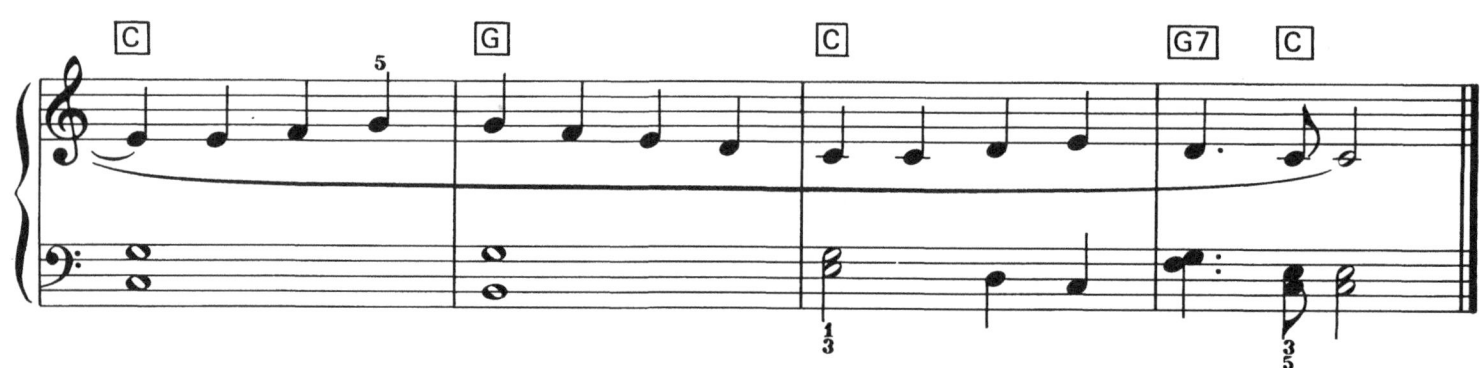

© Copyright MCMLXXXVI by Bosworth & Co.

B. & Co. 24 742

Alle Rechte vorbehalten
All rights reserved

Cancan

aus der Operette "Orpheus in der Unterwelt"

Jacques Offenbach (1819-1880)
Arr.: Hans-Günter Heumann

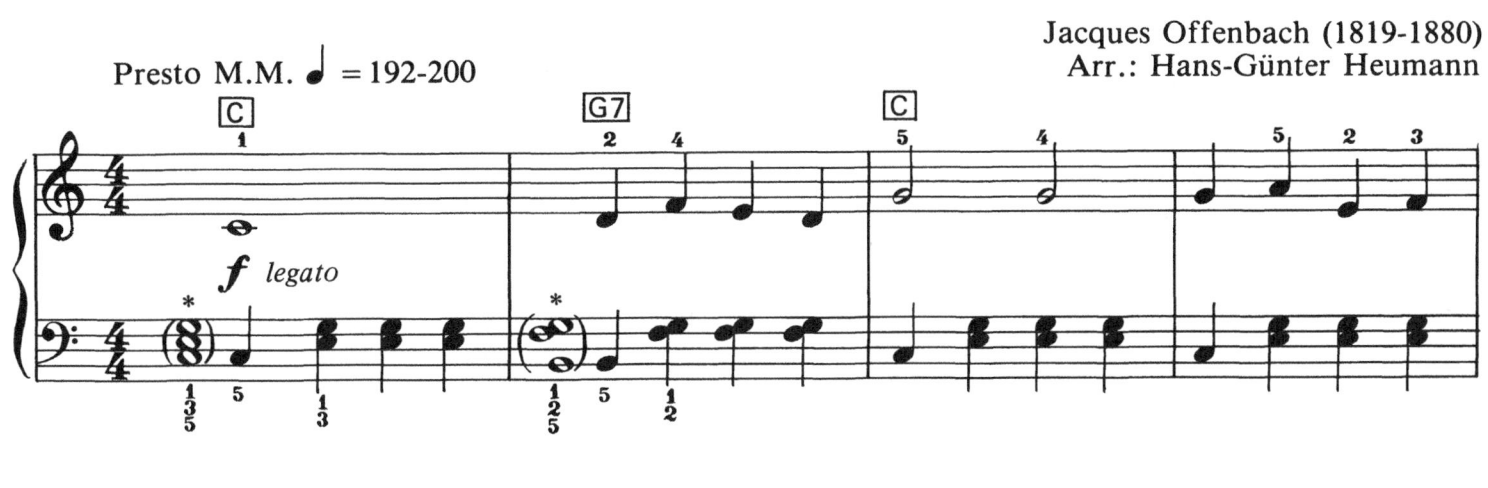

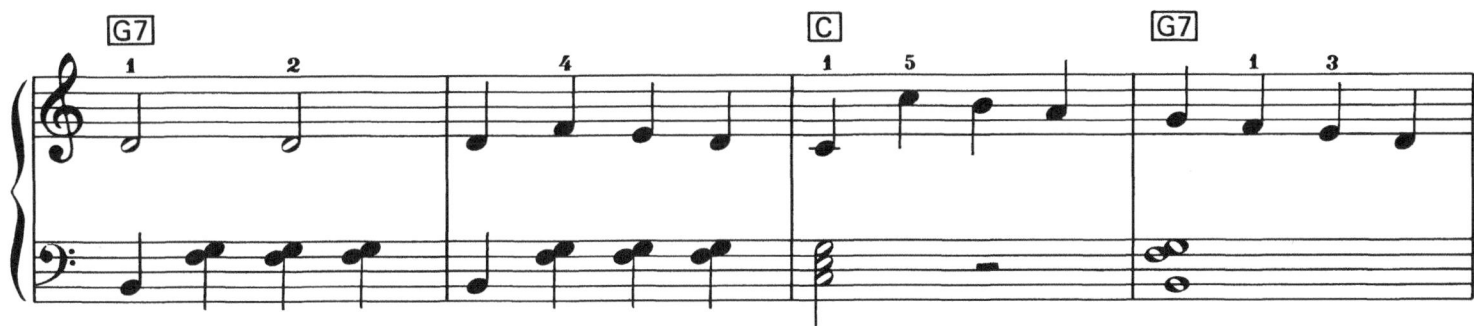

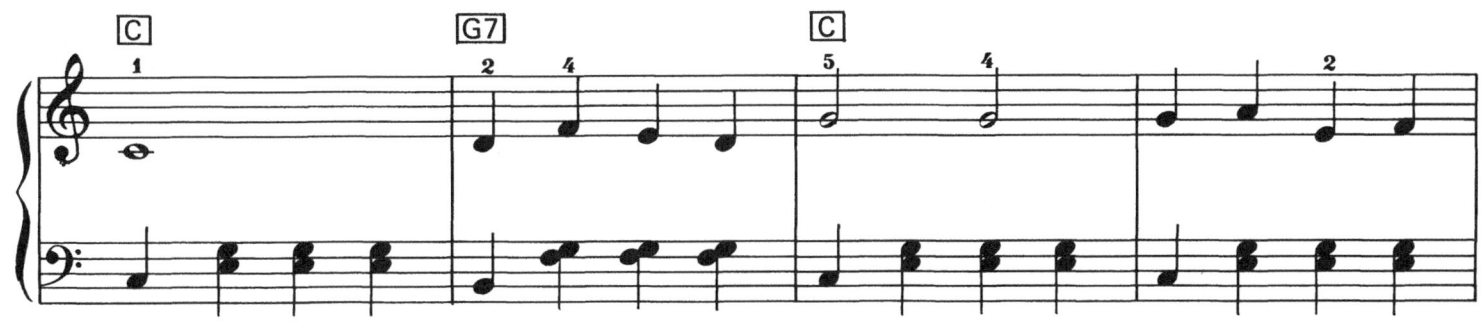

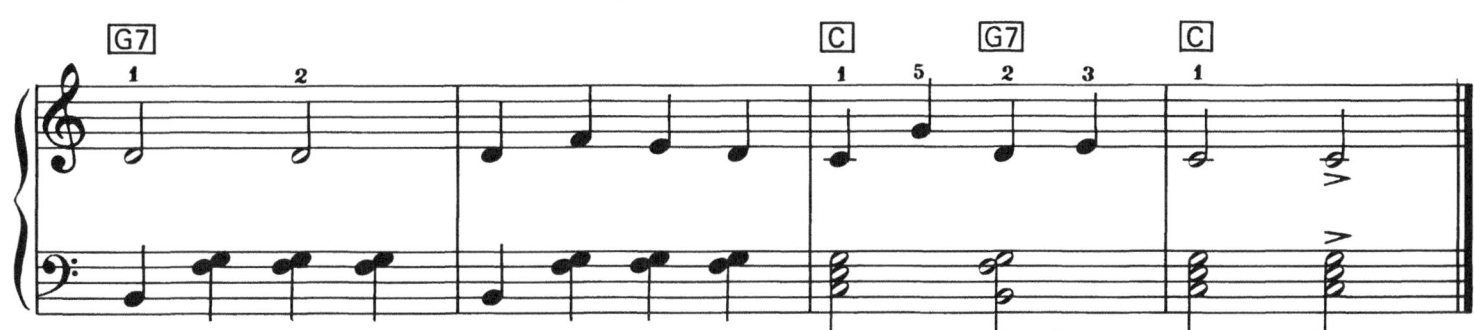

*) Anmerkung für den Lehrer:
Die linke Hand sollte zunächst als Akkordzusammenlegung gespielt werden.

*) Notes for the teacher:
At first, the L.H. should be played as individual complete chords.

© Copyright MCMLXXXVI by Bosworth & Co.

Alle Rechte vorbehalten
All rights reserved

Champagner-Arie
Champagne Aria
aus der Oper "Don Giovanni"

Wolfgang Amadeus Mozart (1756-1791)
Arr.: Hans-Günter Heumann

Brautchor
The Wedding March
aus der Oper "Lohengrin"

Richard Wagner (1813-1883)
Arr.: Hans-Günter Heumann

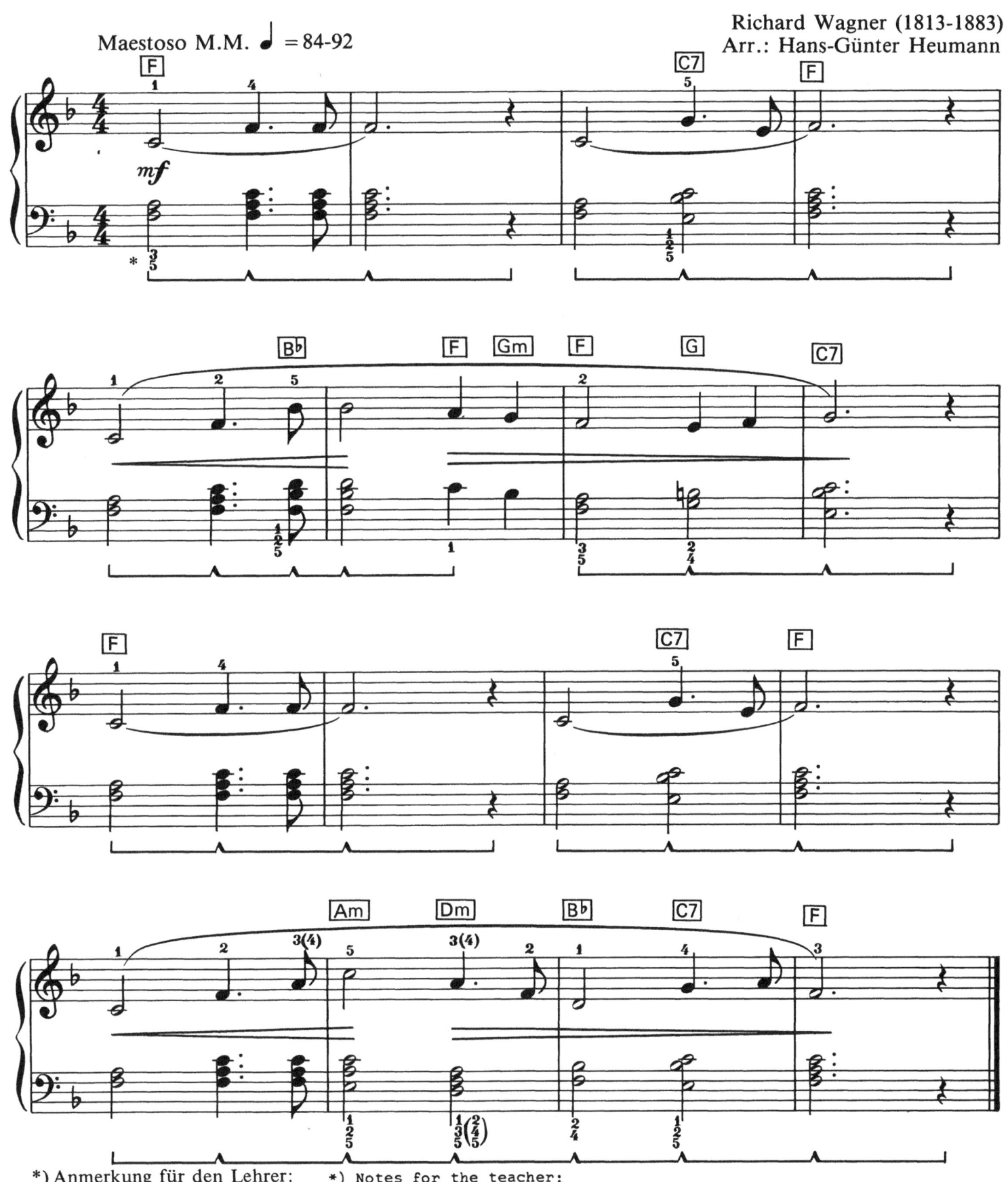

*) Anmerkung für den Lehrer:
Ad lib. senza Pedal.

*) Notes for the teacher:
Ad lib. senza Pedal

© Copyright MCMLXXXVI by Bosworth & Co.

Alle Rechte vorbehalten
All rights reserved

Militärmarsch
Military March

Franz Schubert (1797-1828)
Arr.: Hans-Günter Heumann

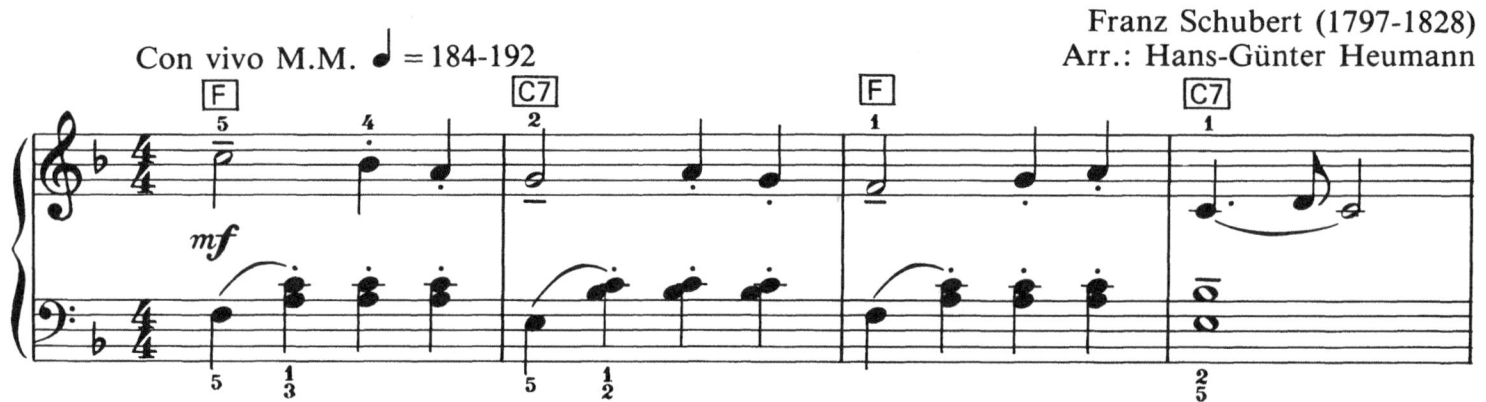
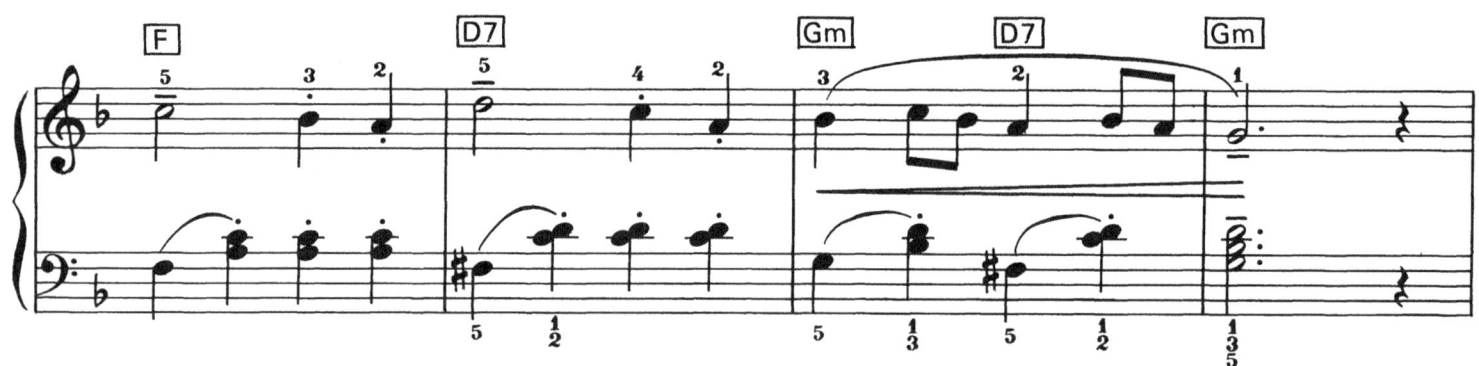
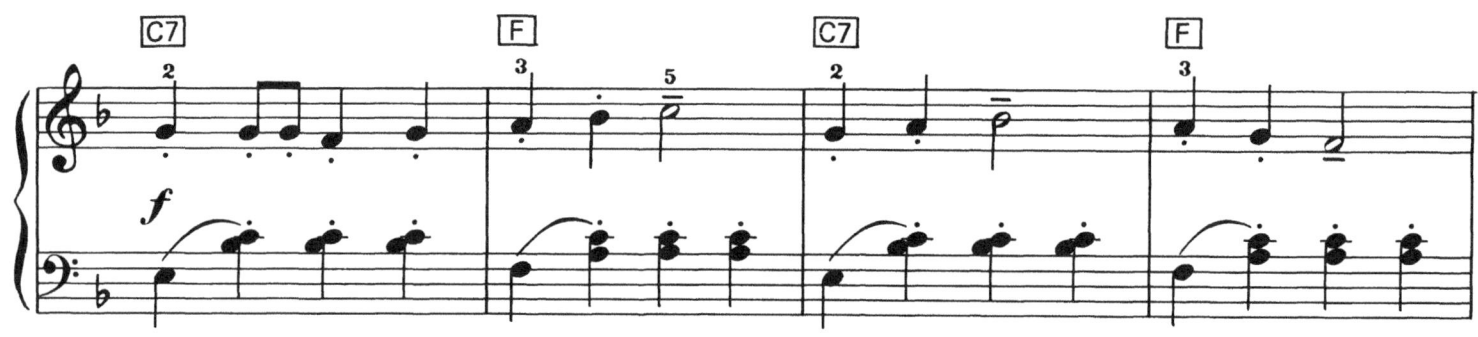
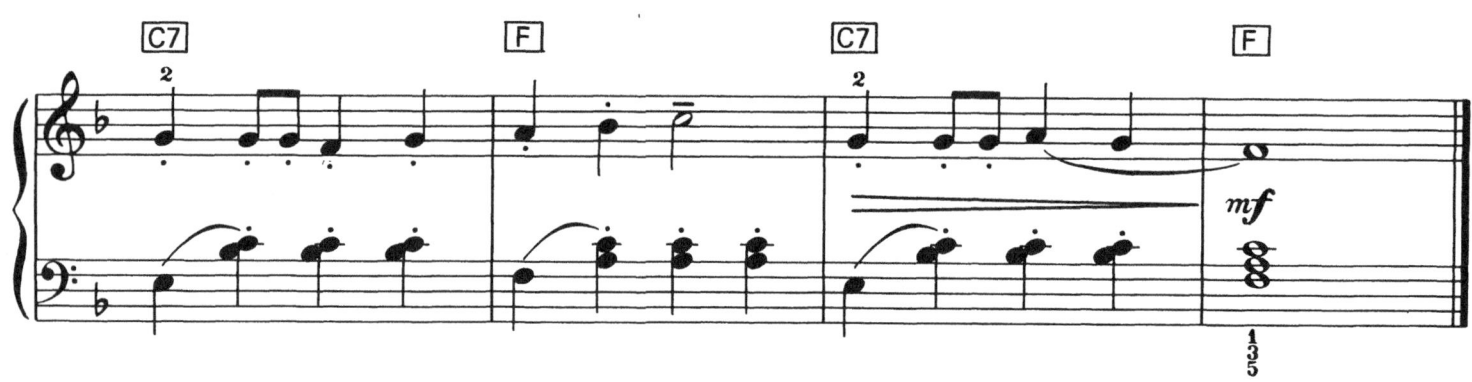

Largo

aus der Sinfonie "Aus der neuen Welt"

Anton Dvořák (1841-1904)
Arr.: Hans-Günter Heumann

Kaiser-Walzer
Emperor Waltz

Johann Strauß, Sohn (1825-1899)
Arr.: Hans-Günter Heumann

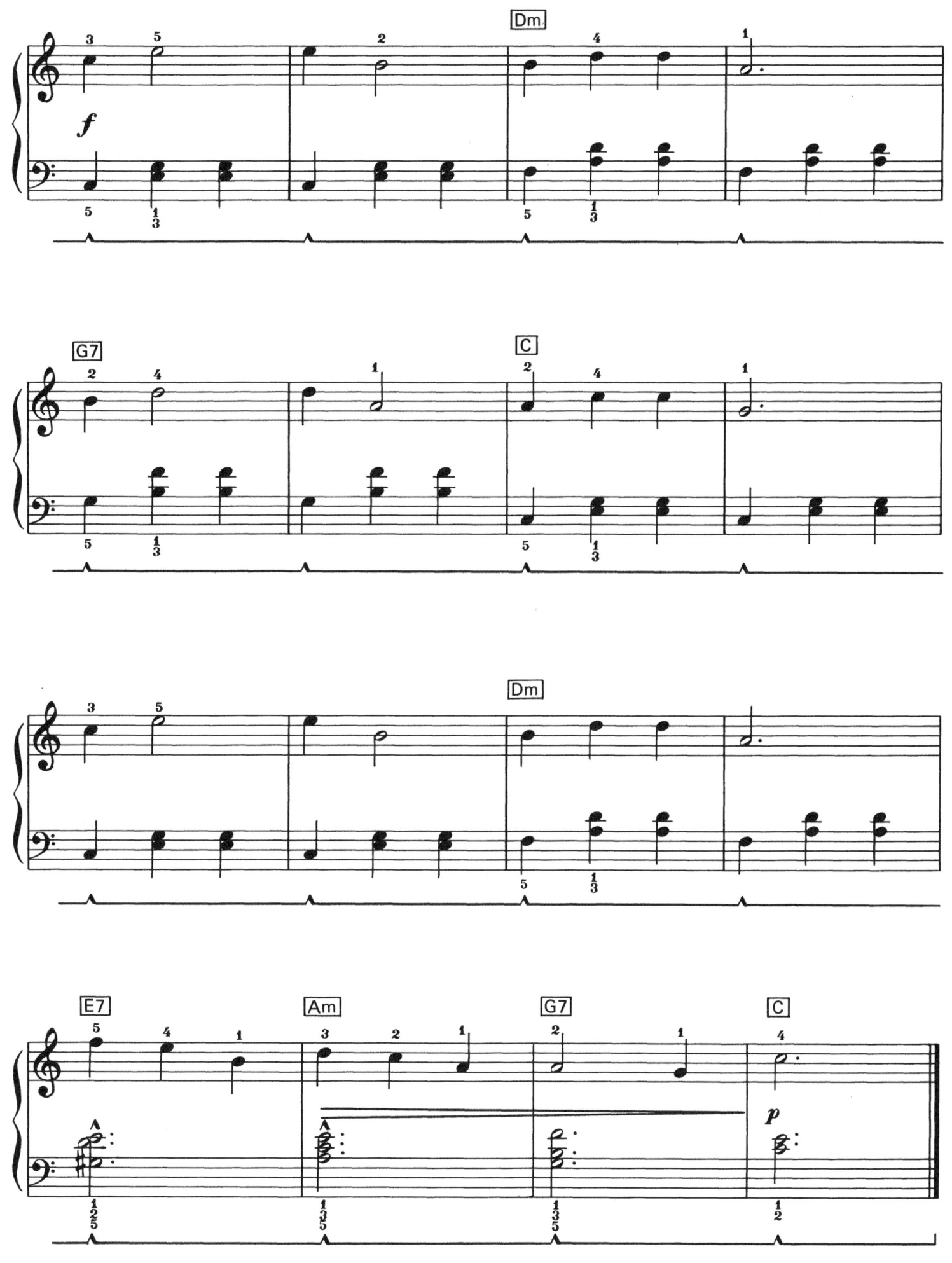

Wiegenlied
Lullaby
Guten Abend, gut' Nacht

*) Anmerkung für den Lehrer:
Ad lib. senza Pedal.

*) Notes for the teacher:
Ad lib. senza Pedal

Für Elise

Klavierstück in a-Moll

Ludwig van Beethoven (1770-1827)
Arr.: Hans-Günter Heumann

*) Anmerkung für den Lehrer:
Pedal ad libitum

An der schönen blauen Donau
The Blue Danube
Walzer-Waltz

Johann Strauß, Sohn (1825-1899)
Arr.: Hans-Günter Heumann

© Copyright MCMLXXXVI by Bosworth & Co.

O wie so trügerisch
La donna è mobile
Arie aus der Oper "Rigoletto"

Giuseppe Verdi (1813-1901)
Arr.: Hans-Günter Heumann

Moderato M.M. ♩ = 116-120

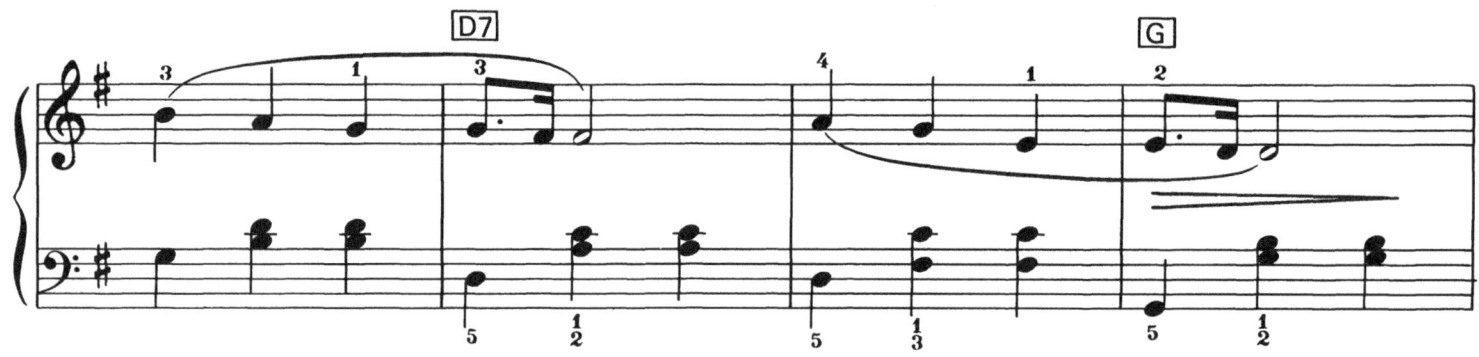

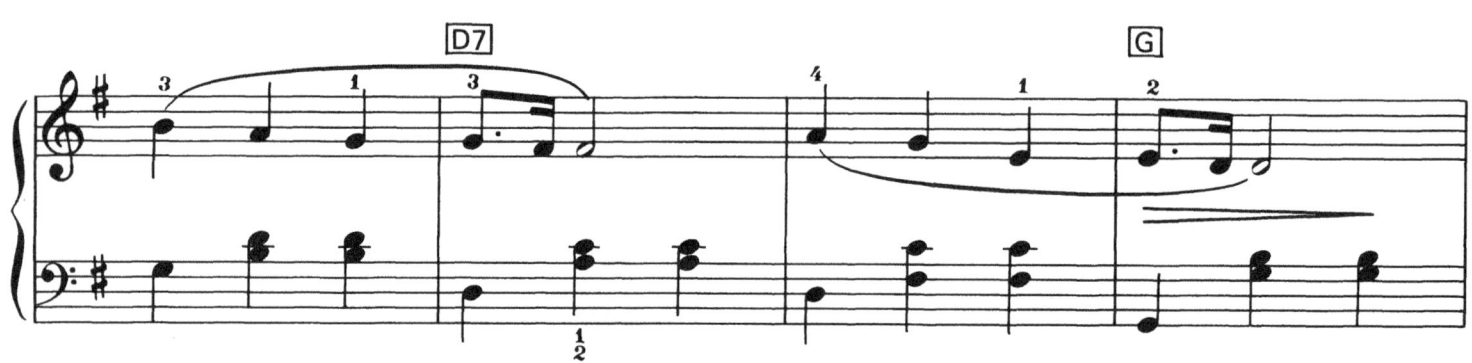

© Copyright MCMLXXXVI by Bosworth & Co.

B. & Co. 24 742

Alle Rechte vorbehalten
All rights reserved

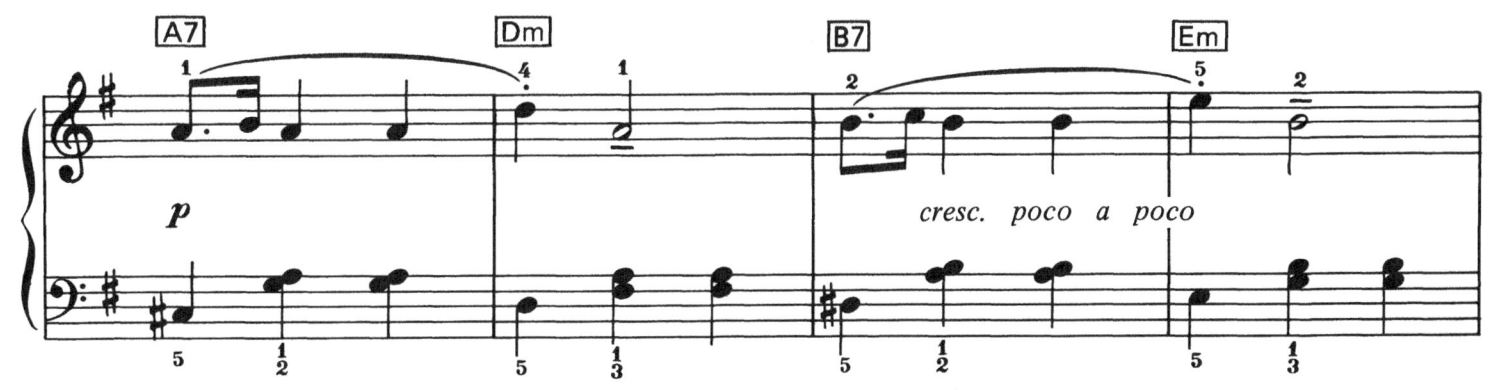
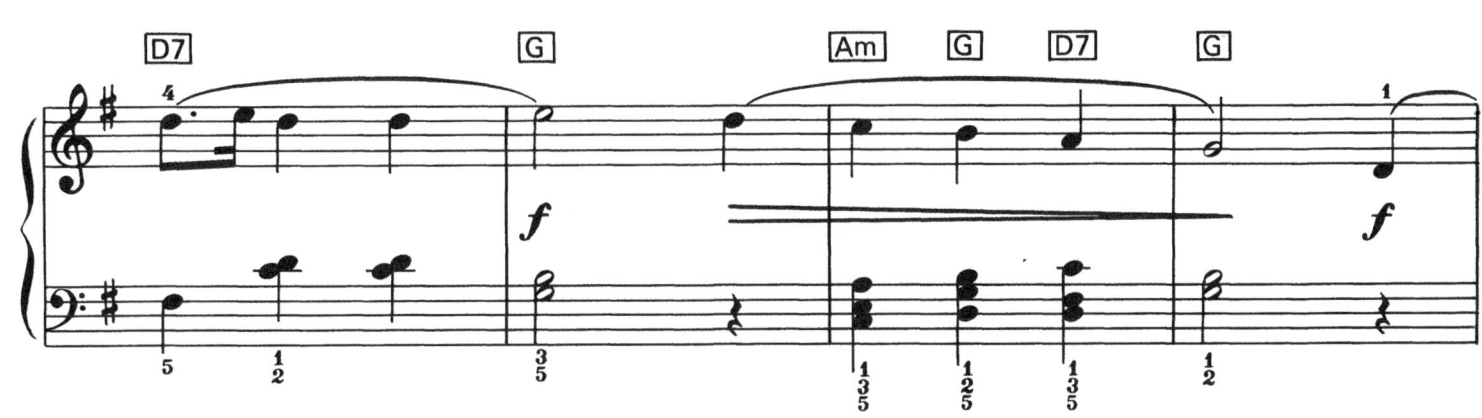
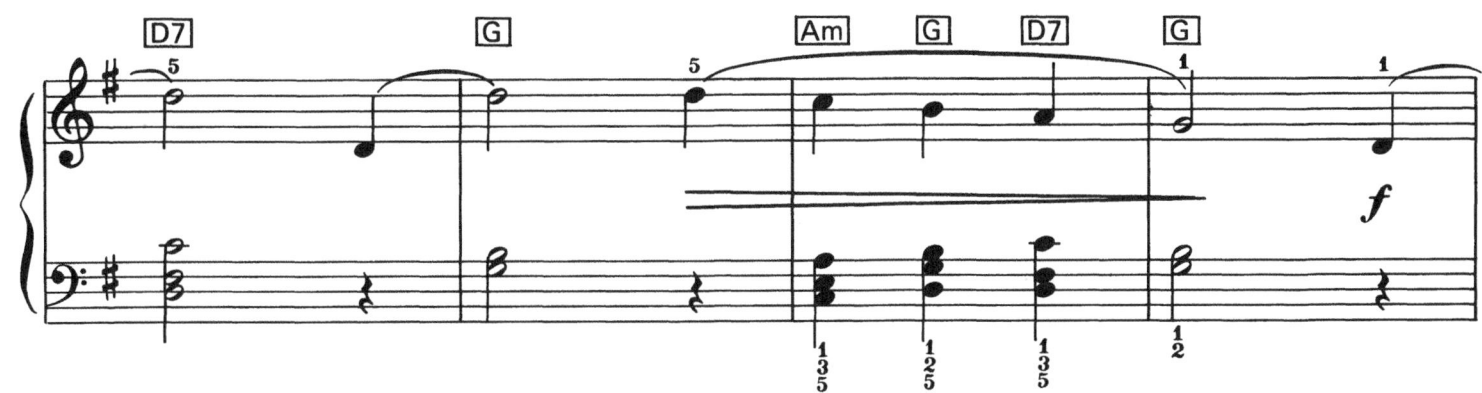
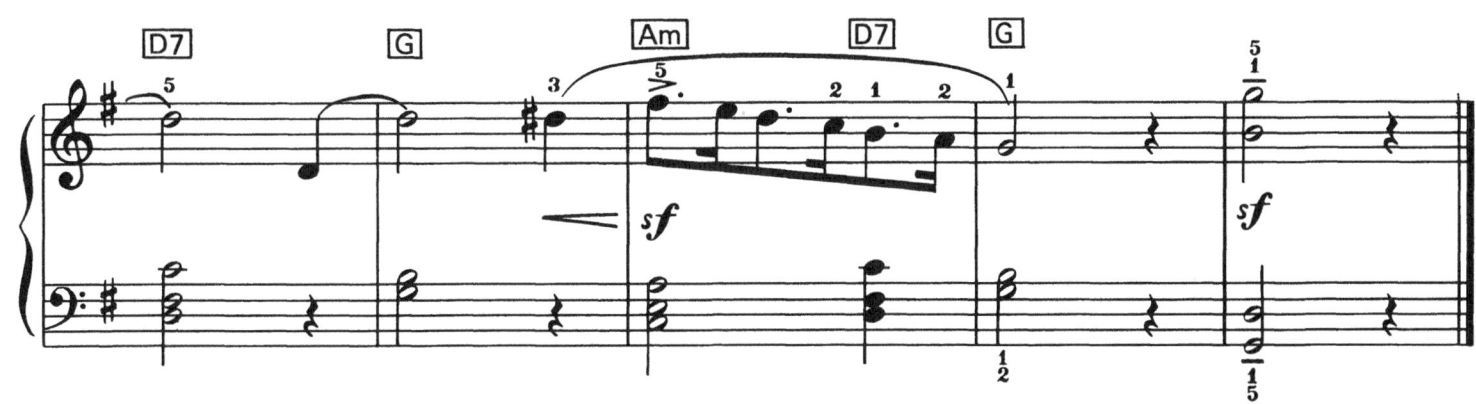

Menuett
Minuet

Jean-Philippe Rameau (1683-1764)
Arr.: Hans-Günter Heumann

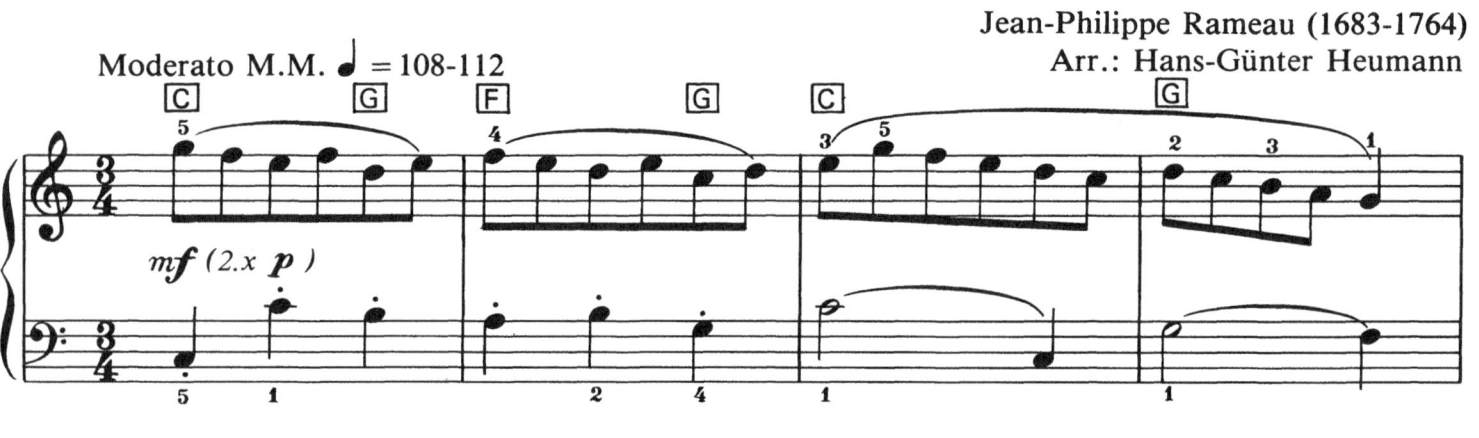
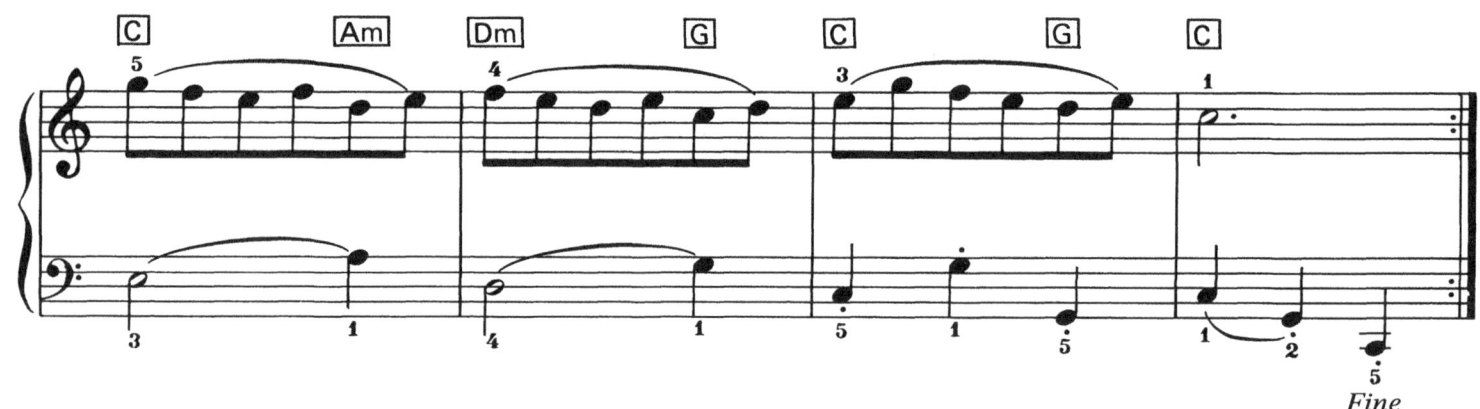
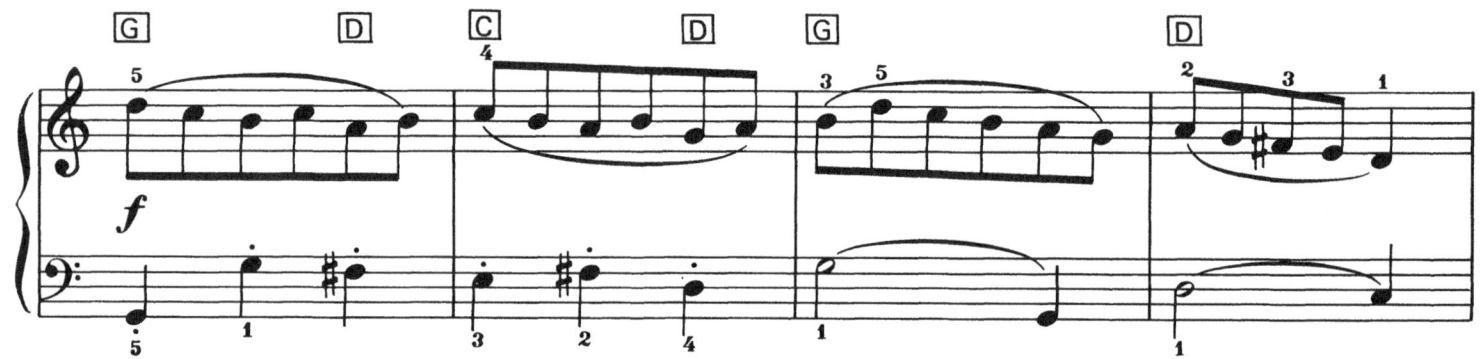
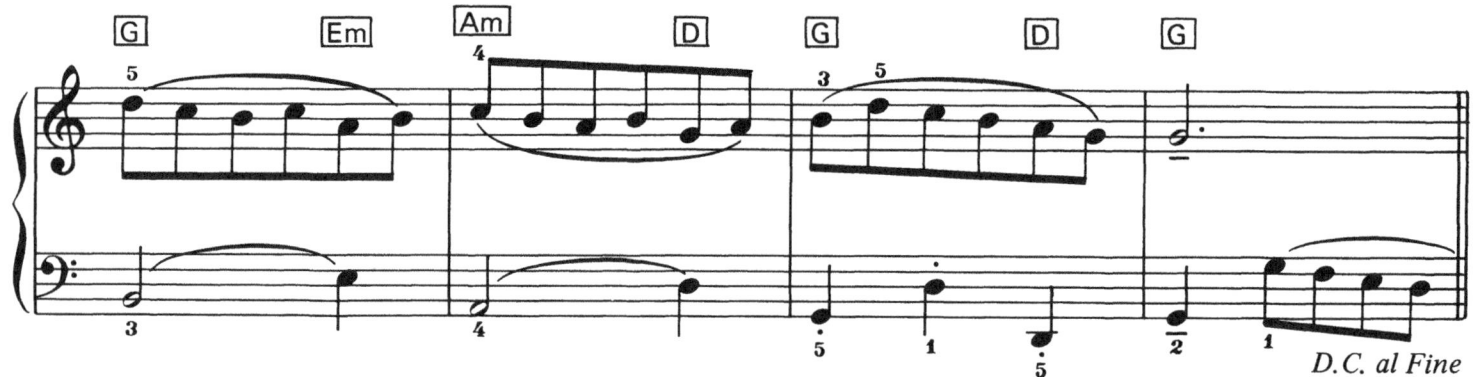

Deutscher Tanz
German Dance

Ludwig van Beethoven (1770-1827)

Sehnsuchtswalzer
Longing

Franz Schubert (1797-1828)
Arr.: Hans-Günter Heumann

Menuett
Minuet

Wolfgang Amadeus Mozart (1756-1791)
(KV 2)

Gefangenenchor
Captives' Chorus
aus der Oper "Nabucco"

Giuseppe Verdi (1813-1901)
Arr.: Hans-Günter Heumann

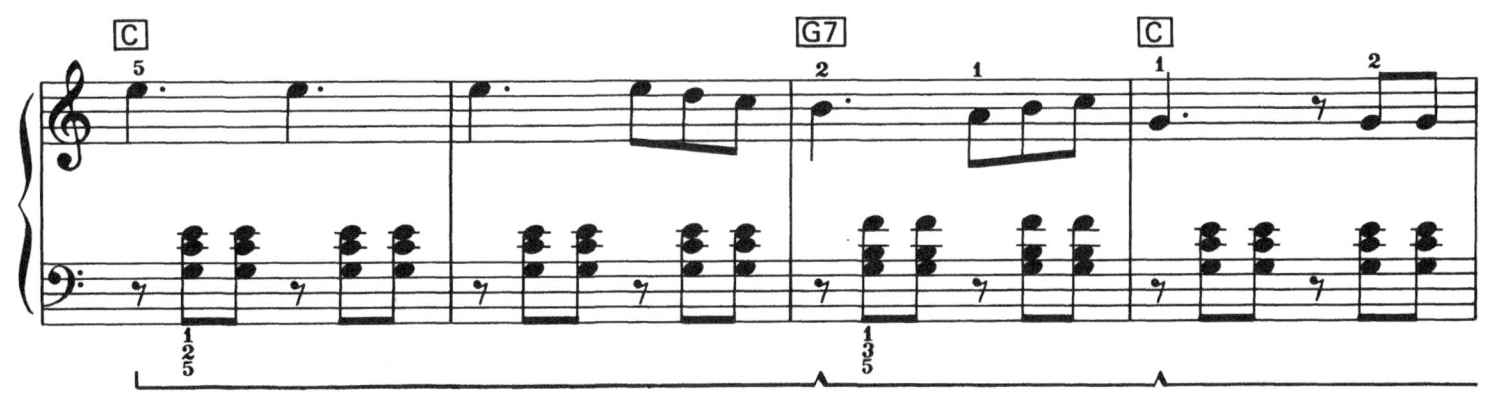
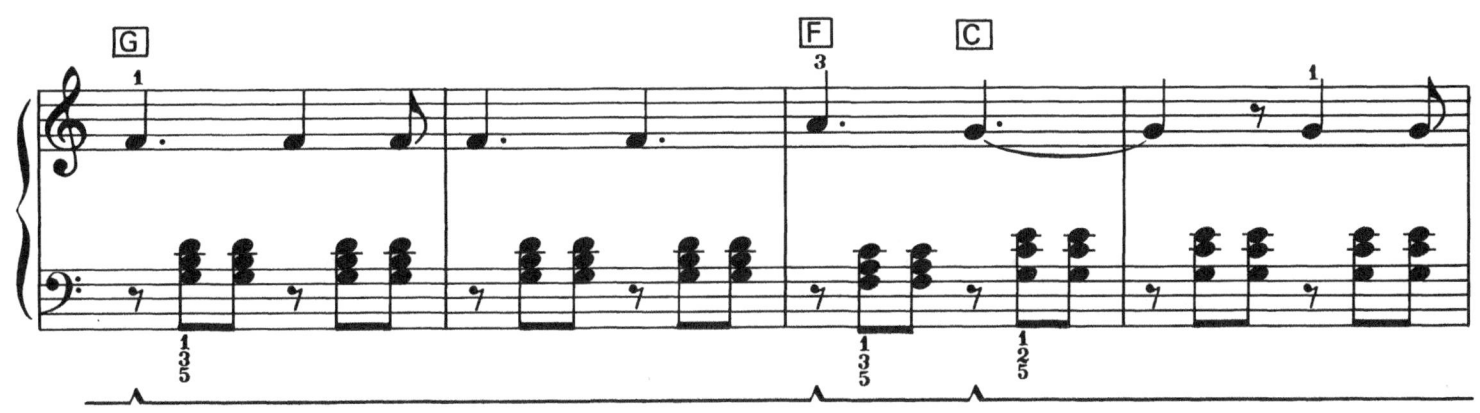

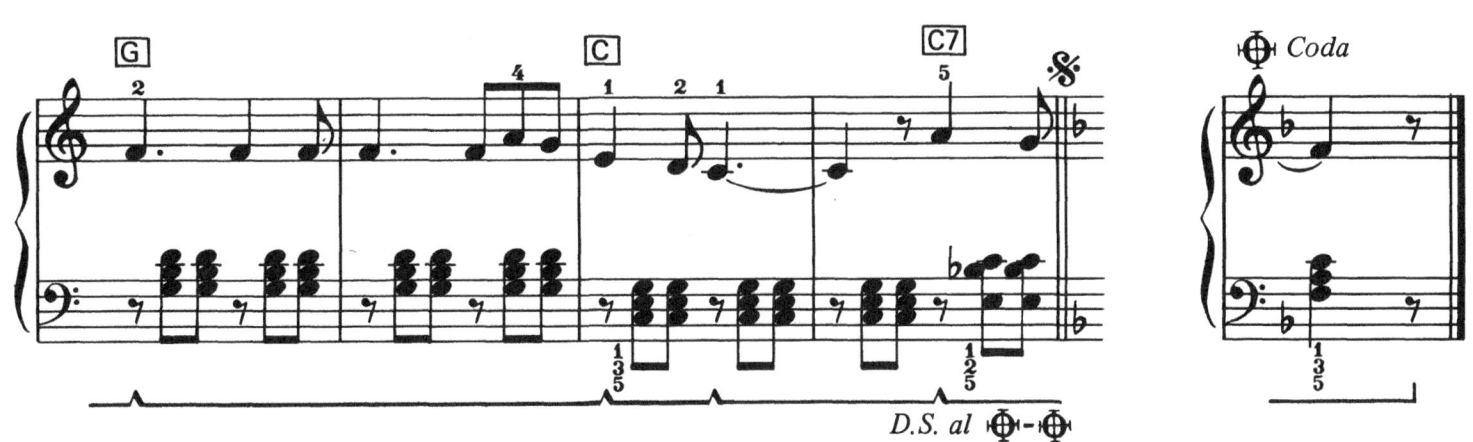

Menuett
Minuet
aus dem "Notenbüchlein für Anna Magdalena Bach"

Johann Sebastian Bach (1685-1750)
BWV Anh. 114

Moderato M.M. ♩ = 108

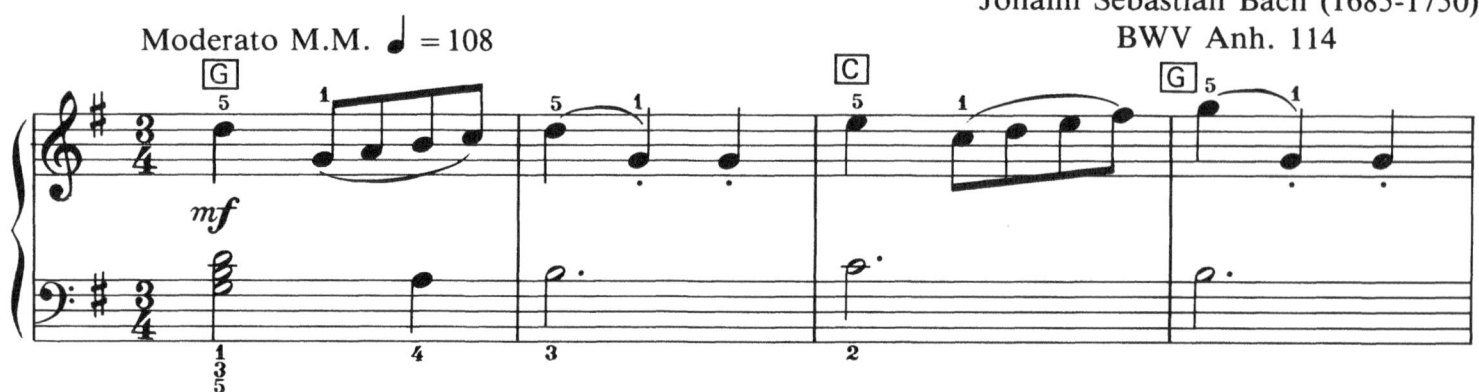

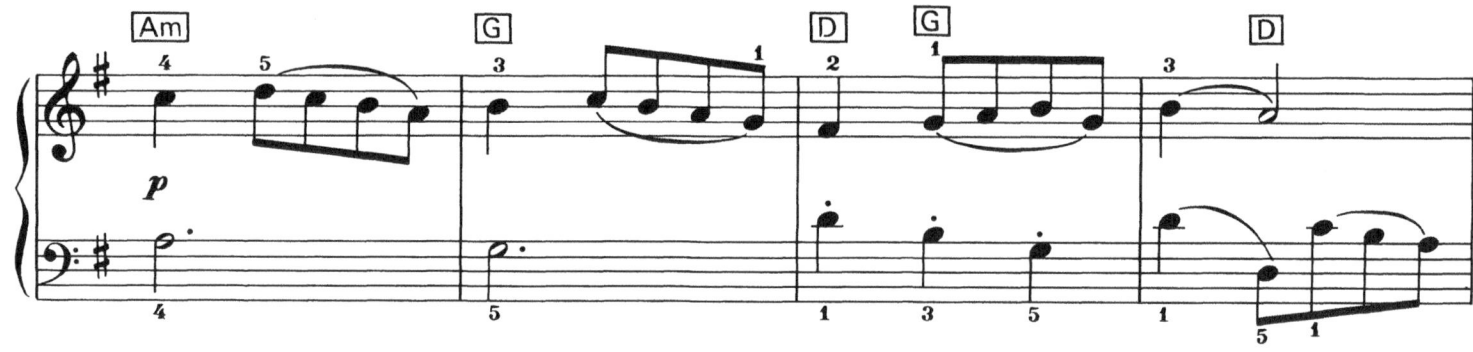

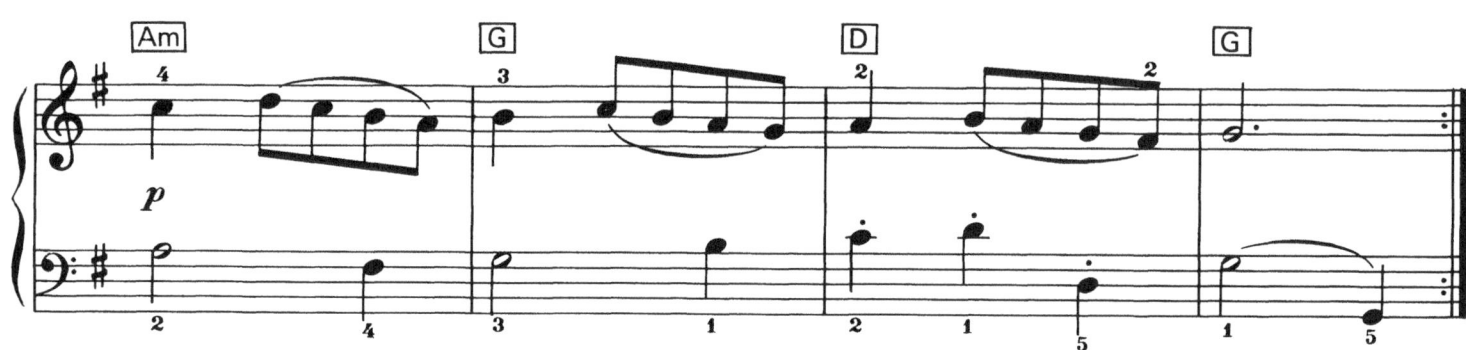

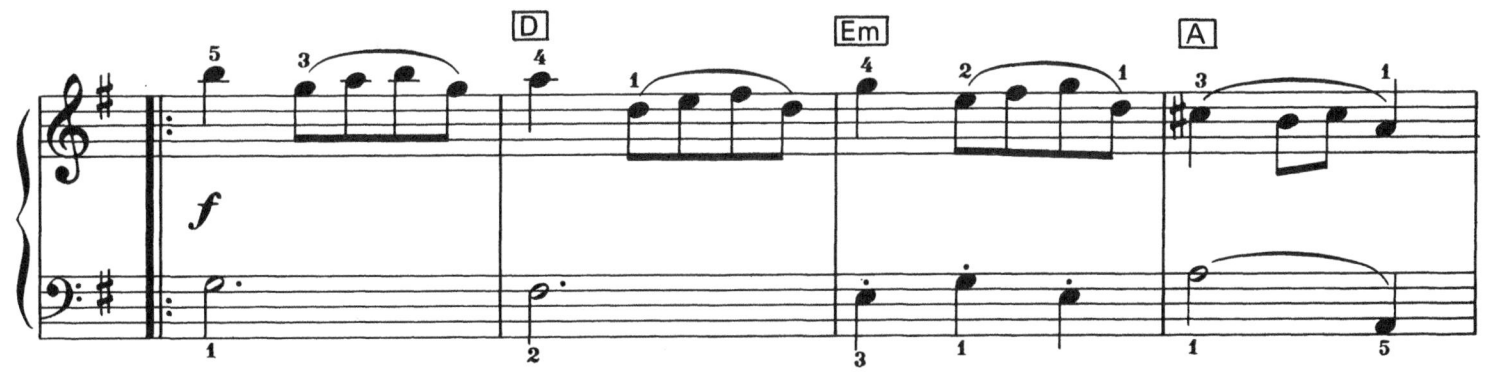
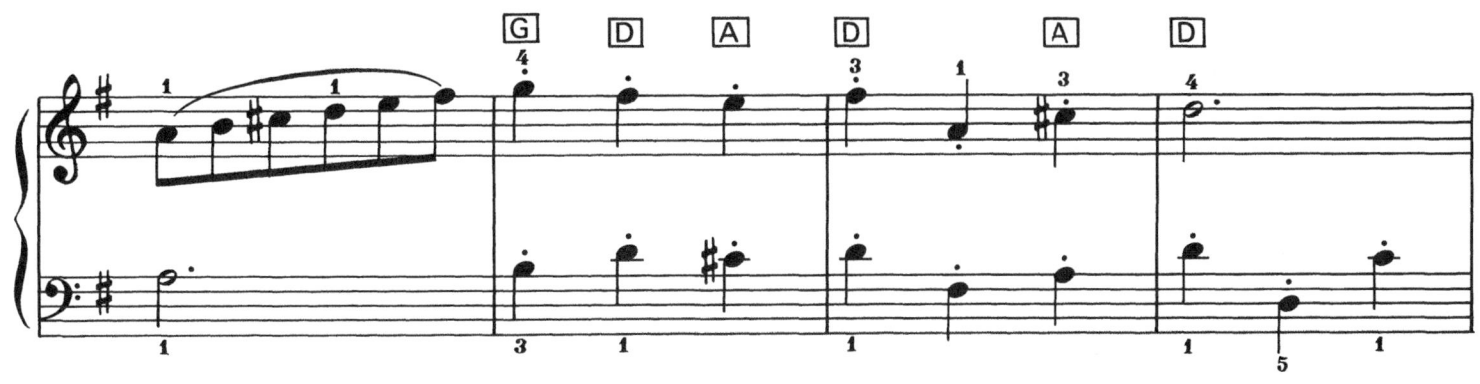
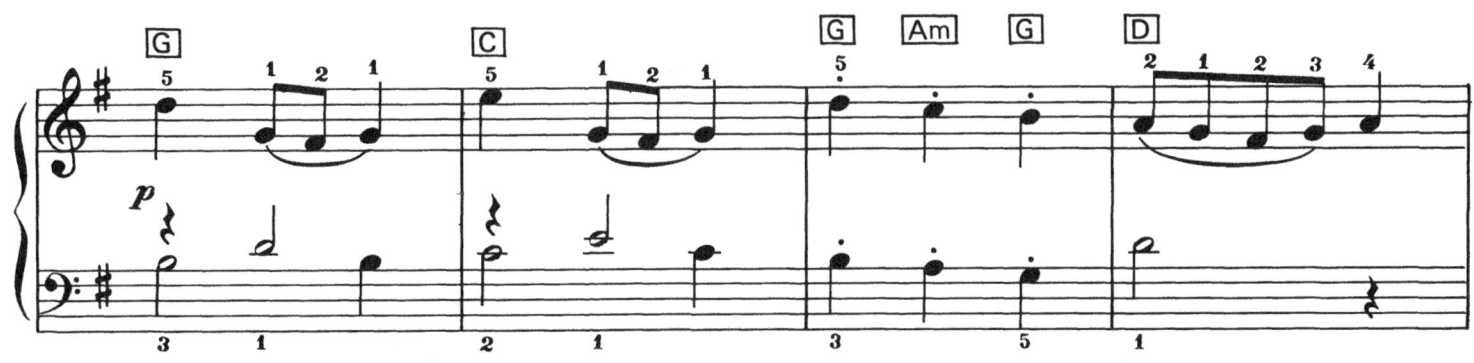
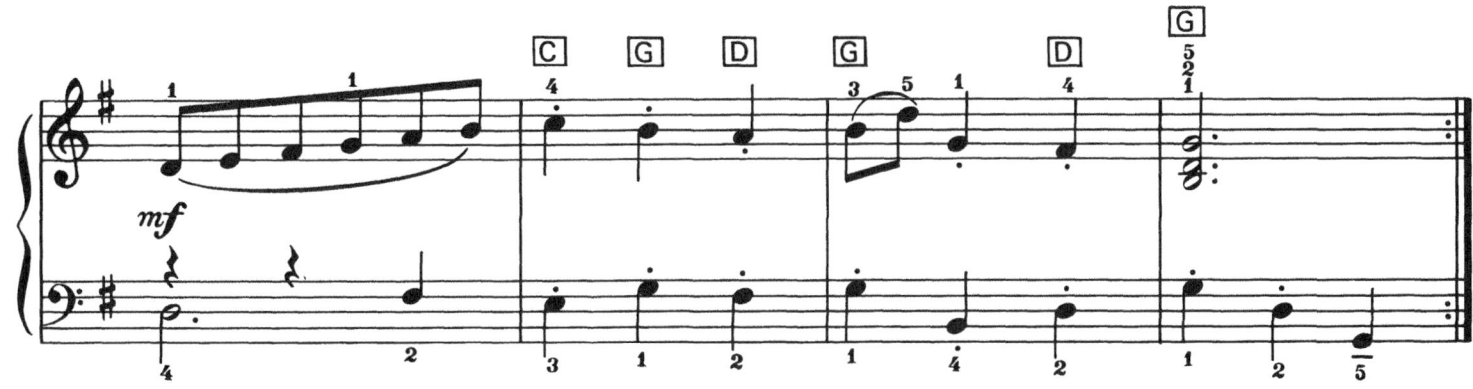

Plaisir d'amour
Romanze

Jean Martini (1741-1816)
Arr.: Hans-Günter Heumann

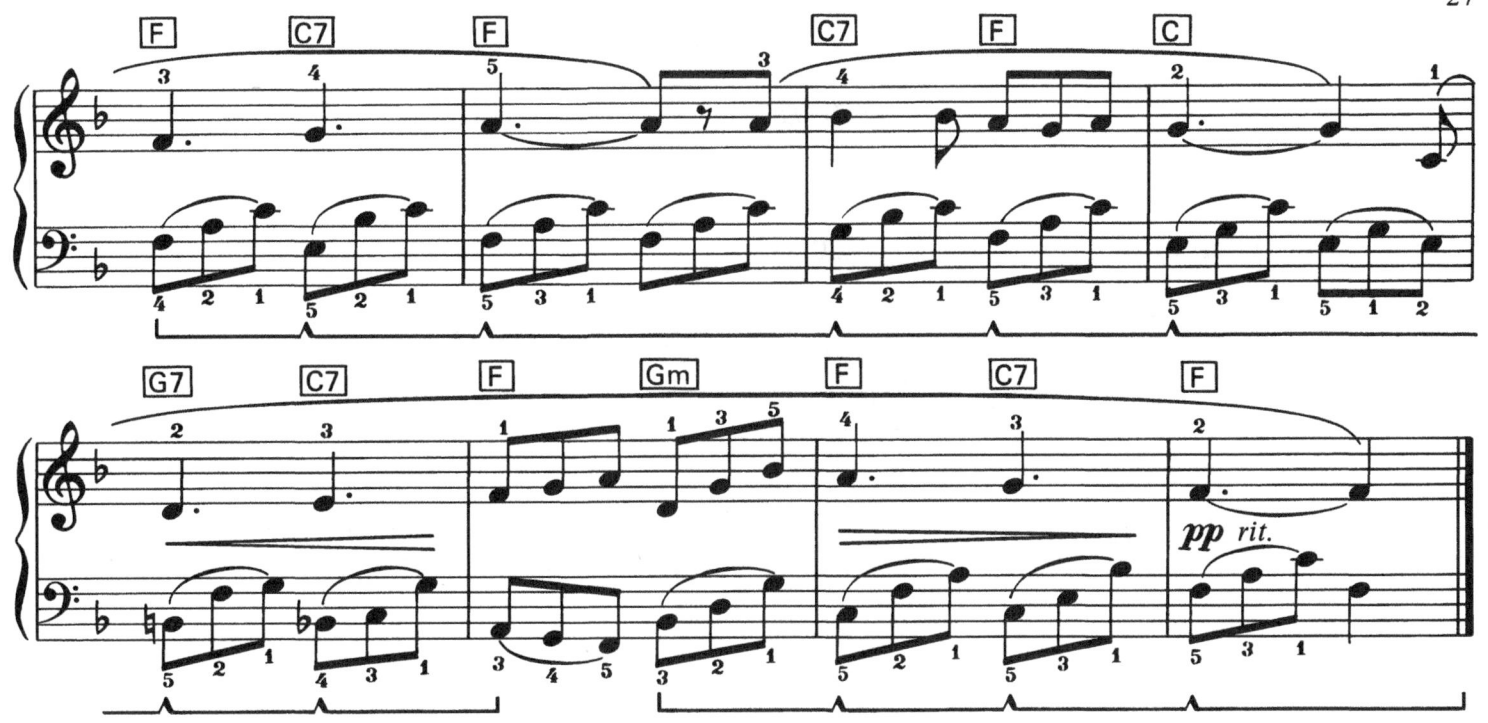

Marsch

March

aus der Oper "Carmen"

Georges Bizet (1838-1875)
Arr.: Hans-Günter Heumann

Allegro con fuoco M.M. ♩ = 120-126

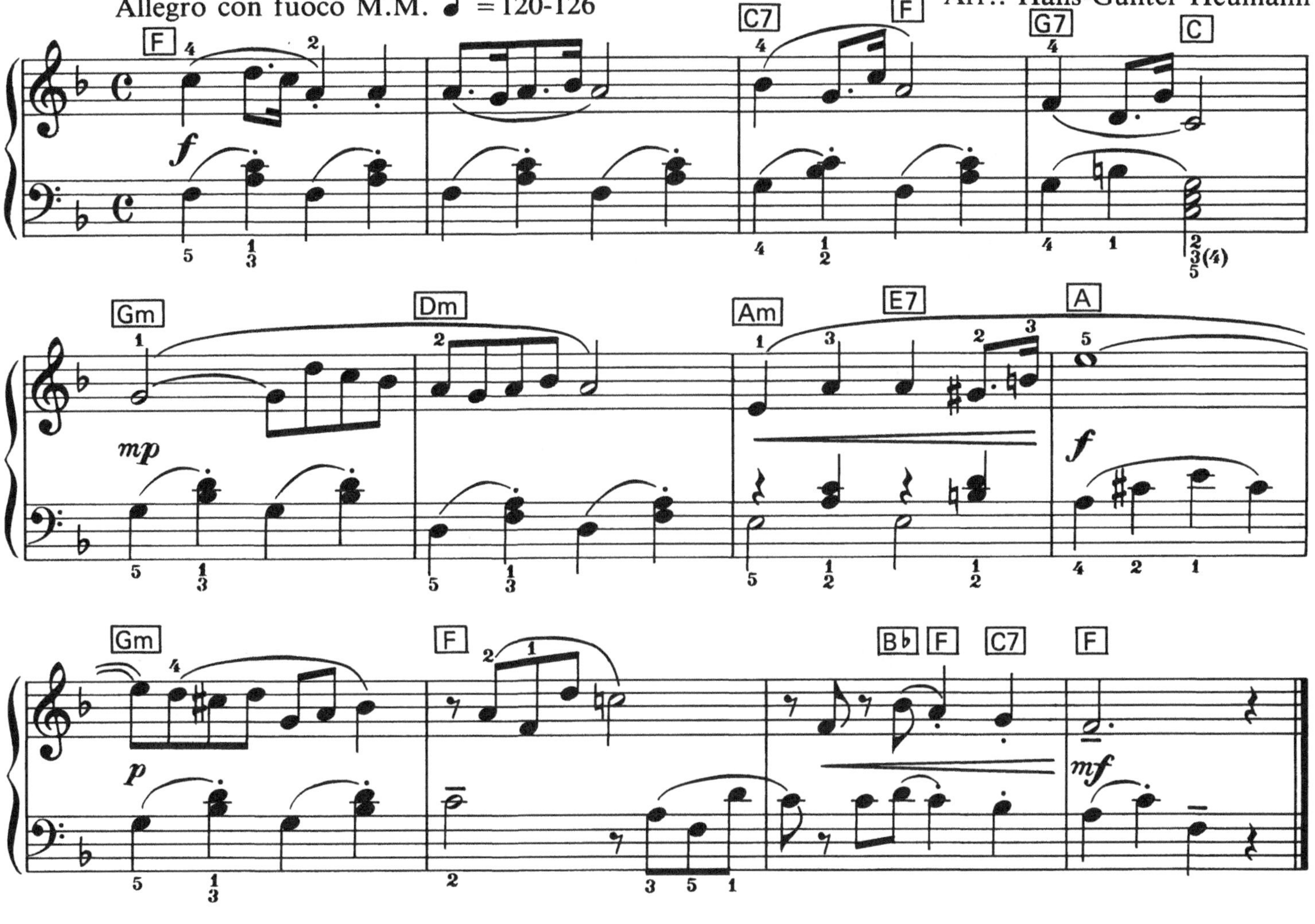

Eine kleine Nachtmusik
Serenade KV 525

Wolfgang Amadeus Mozart (1756-1791)
Arr.: Hans-Günter Heumann

Allegro, ma non troppo M.M. ♩ = 120

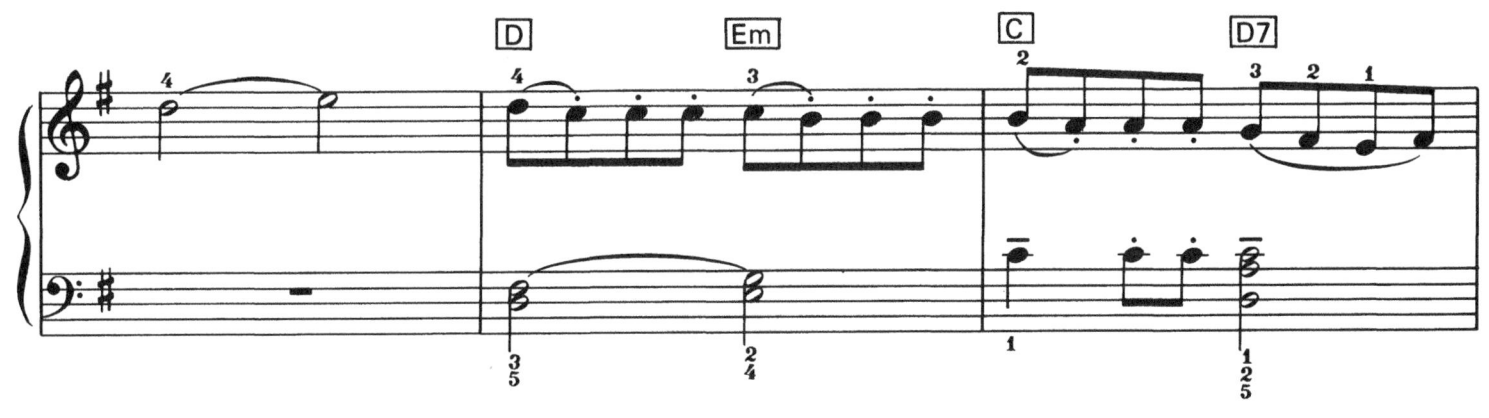
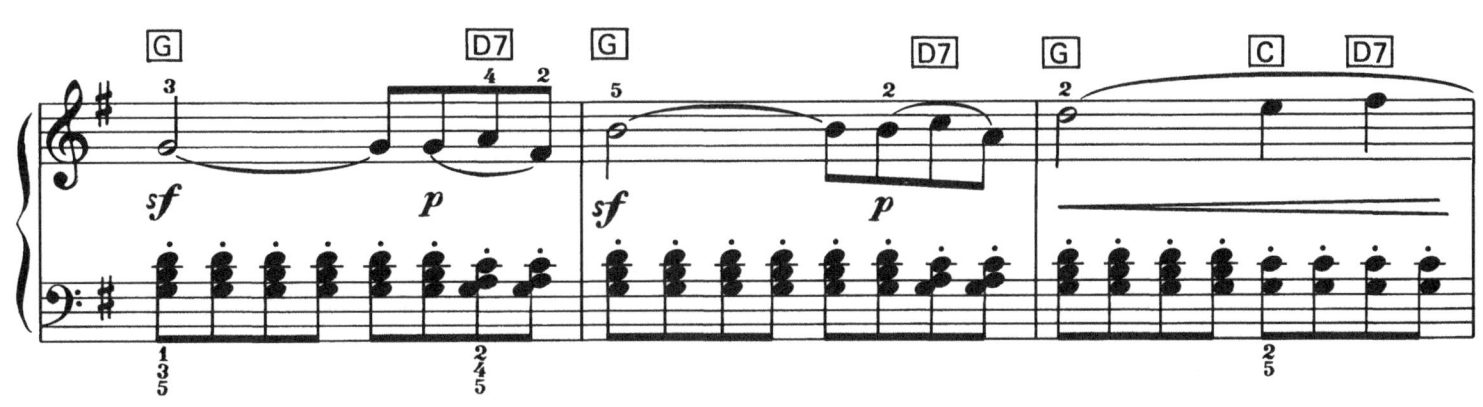
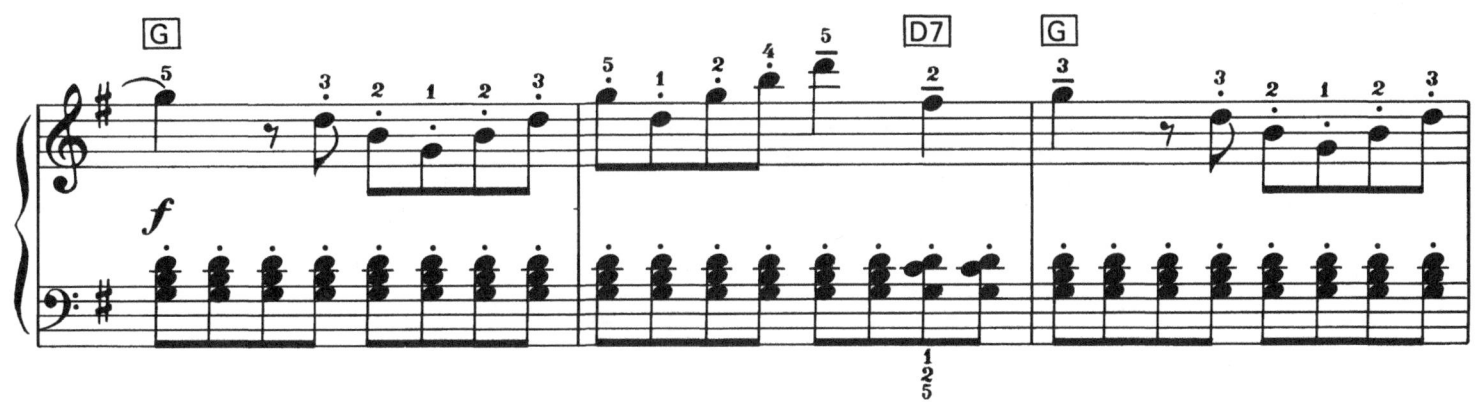
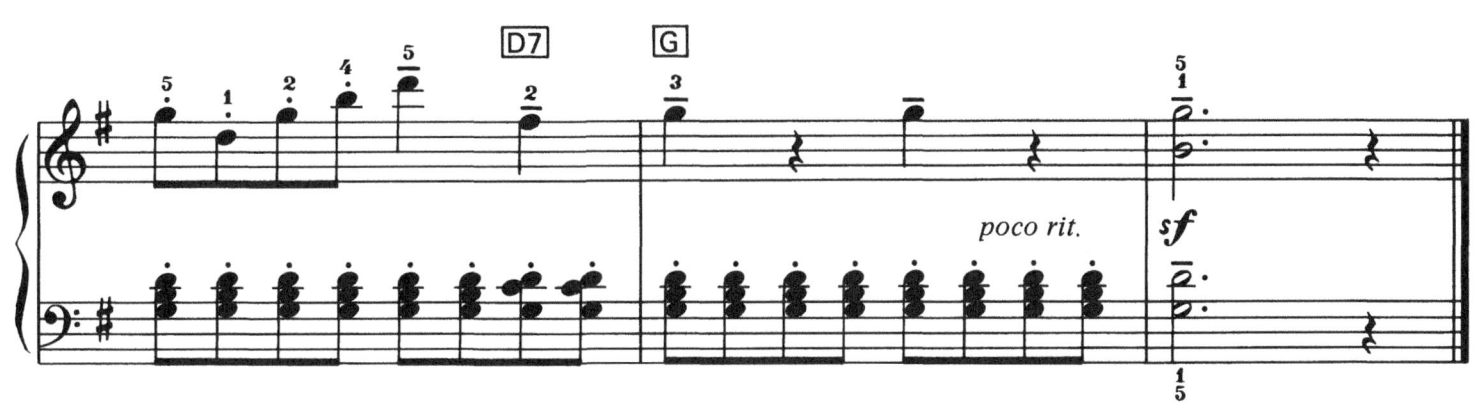

Tristesse

Etüde op. 10, Nr. 3

Frédéric Chopin (1810-1849)
Arr.: Hans-Günter Heumann

Liebestraum

Notturno Nr. 3

Franz Liszt (1811-1886)
Arr.: Hans-Günter Heumann

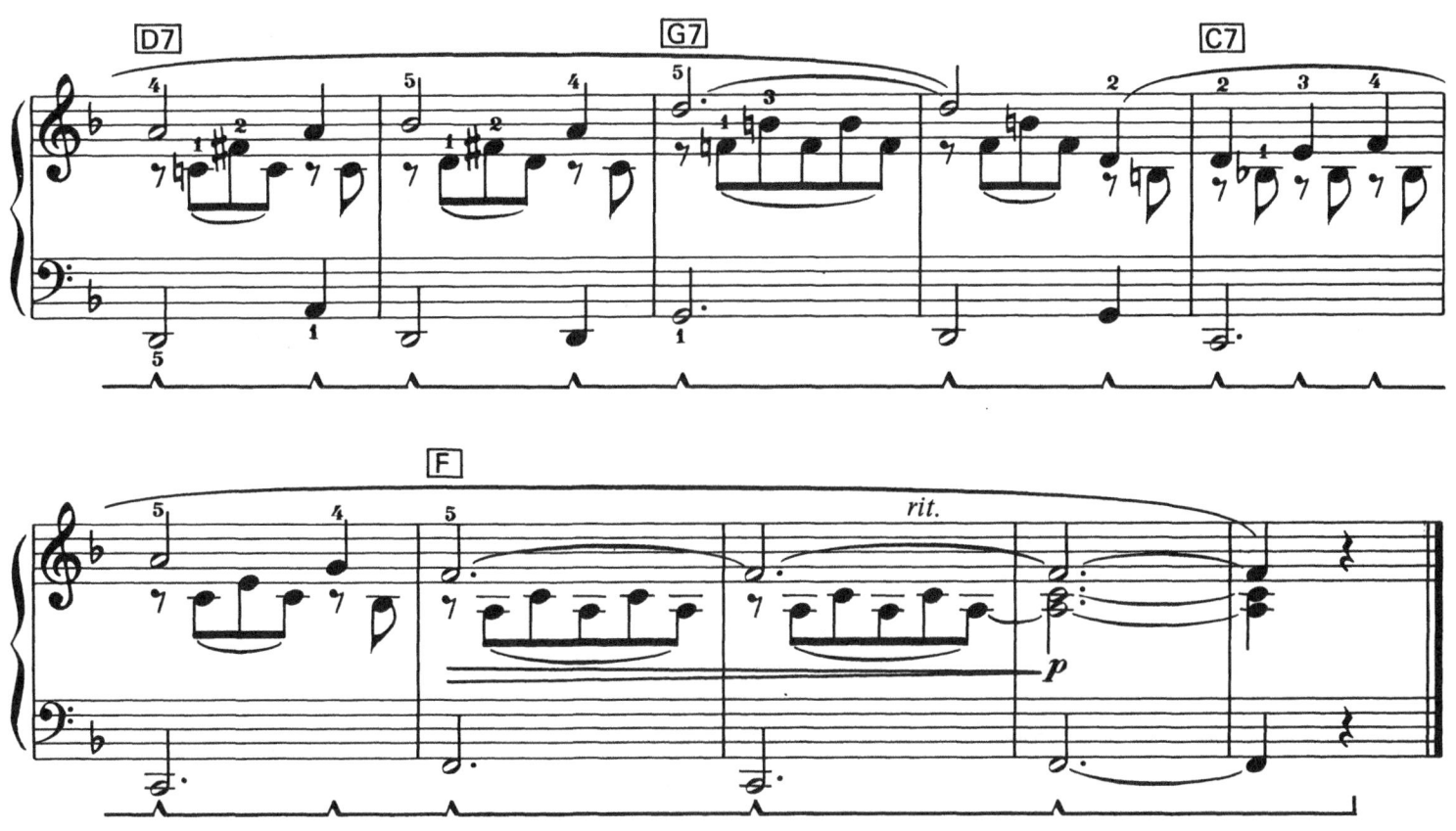

Ecossaise

Franz Schubert (1797-1828)
op. 18, Nr. 4-DV 145

Allegretto M.M. ♩ = 120-126

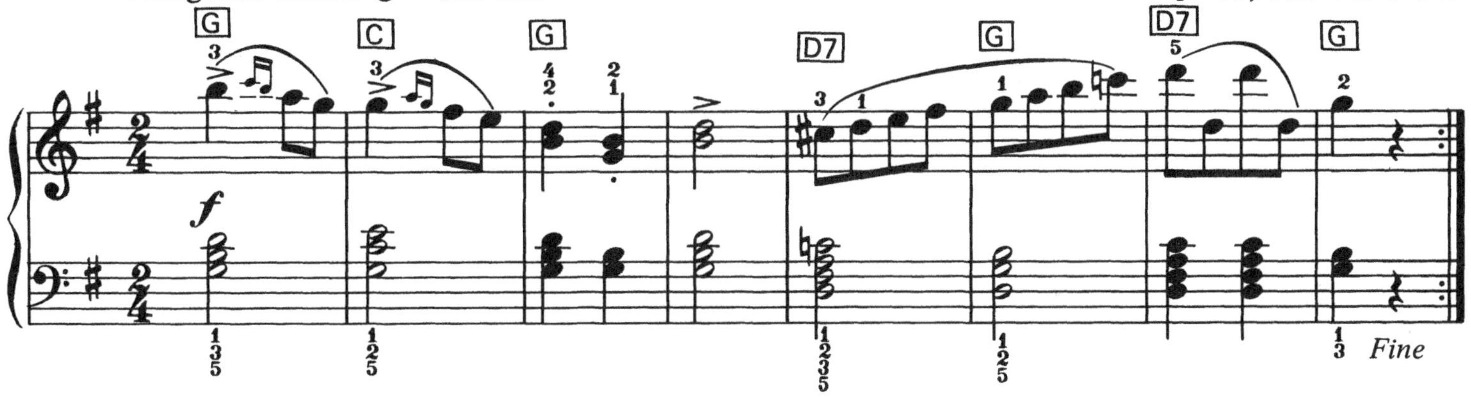

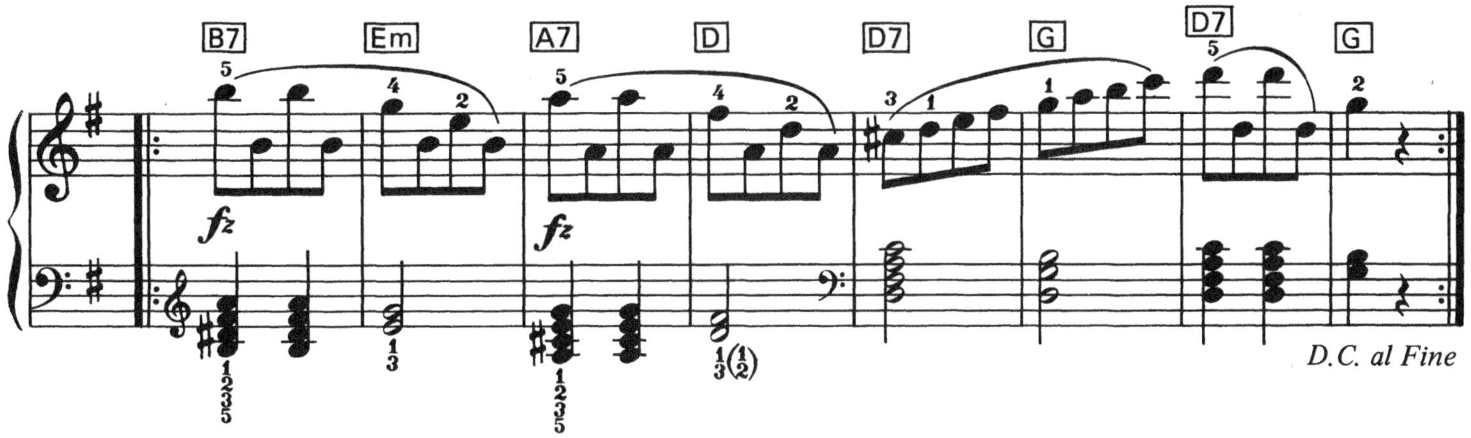

Rondo alla turca
Turkish Rondo
aus der Klaviersonate A-dur, KV 331

Wolfgang Amadeus Mozart (1756-1791)
Arr.: Hans-Günter Heumann

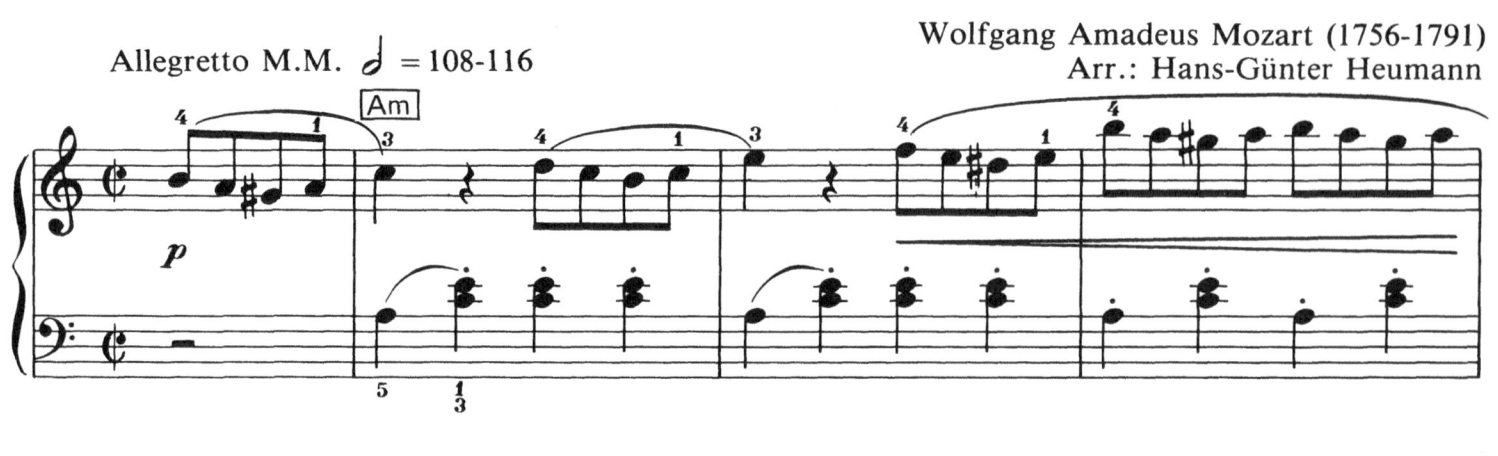

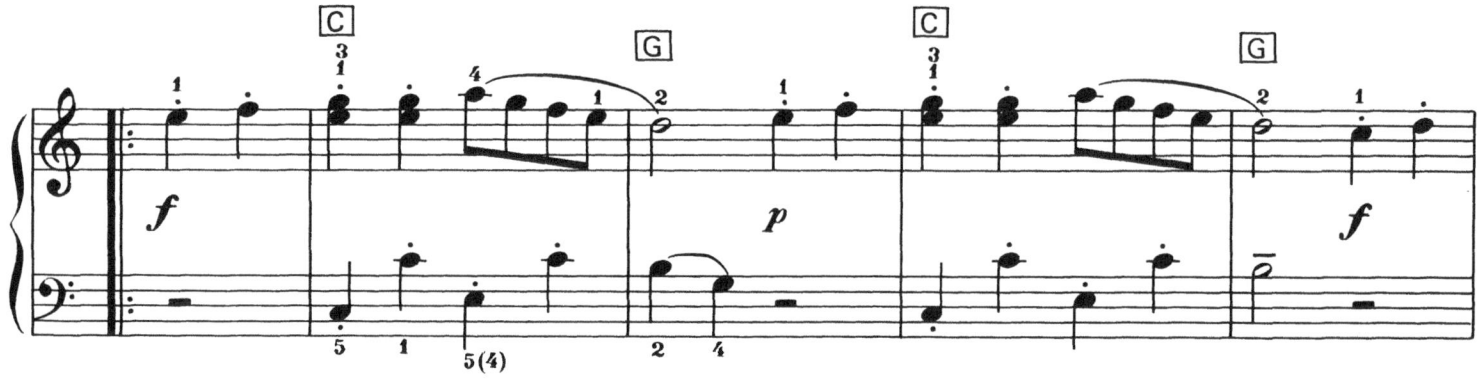

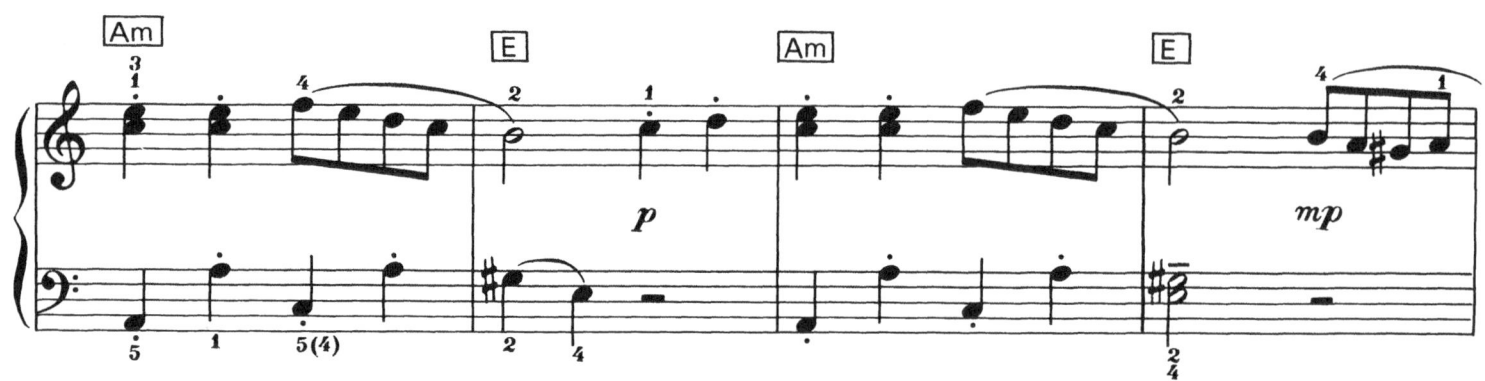

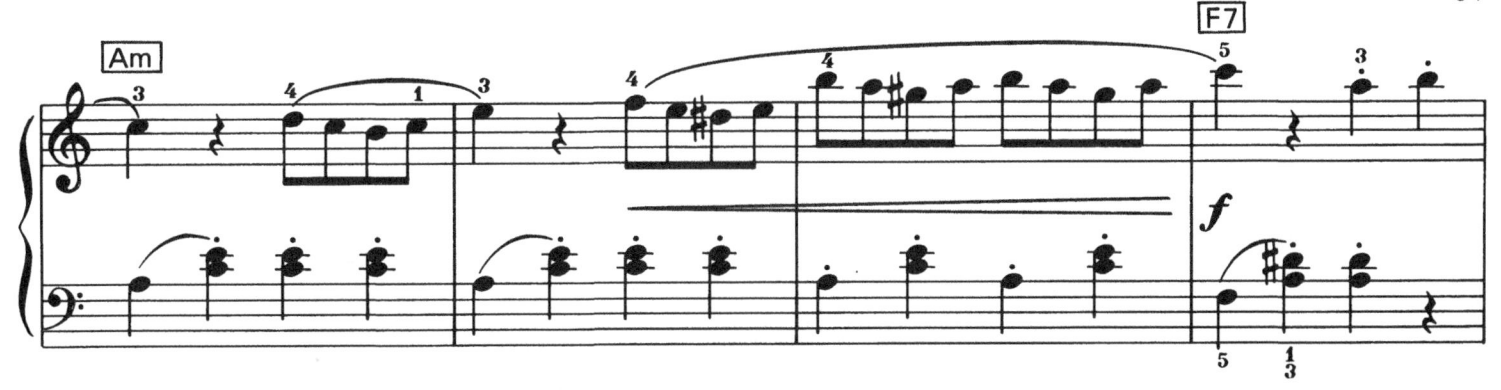
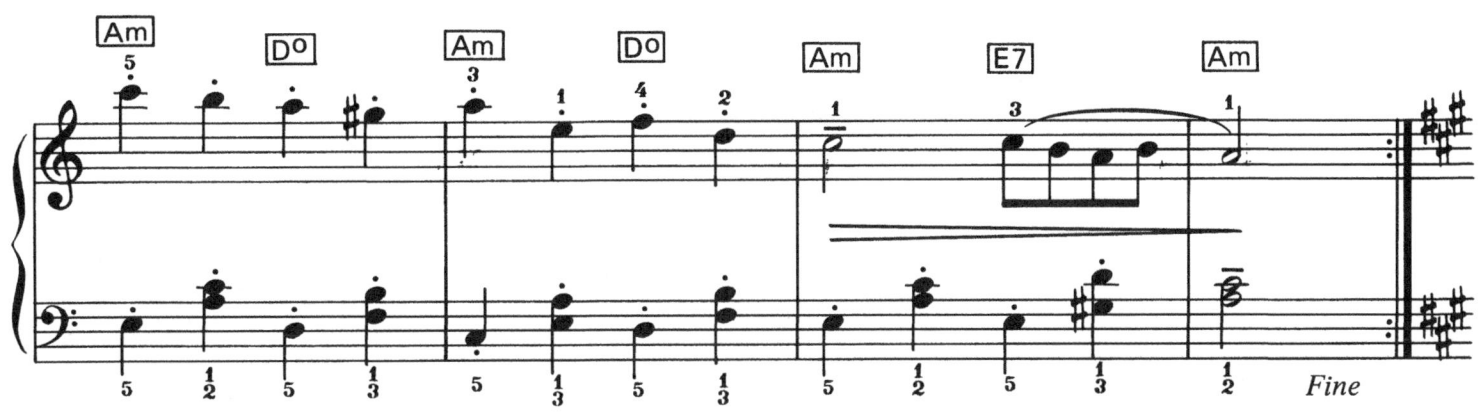
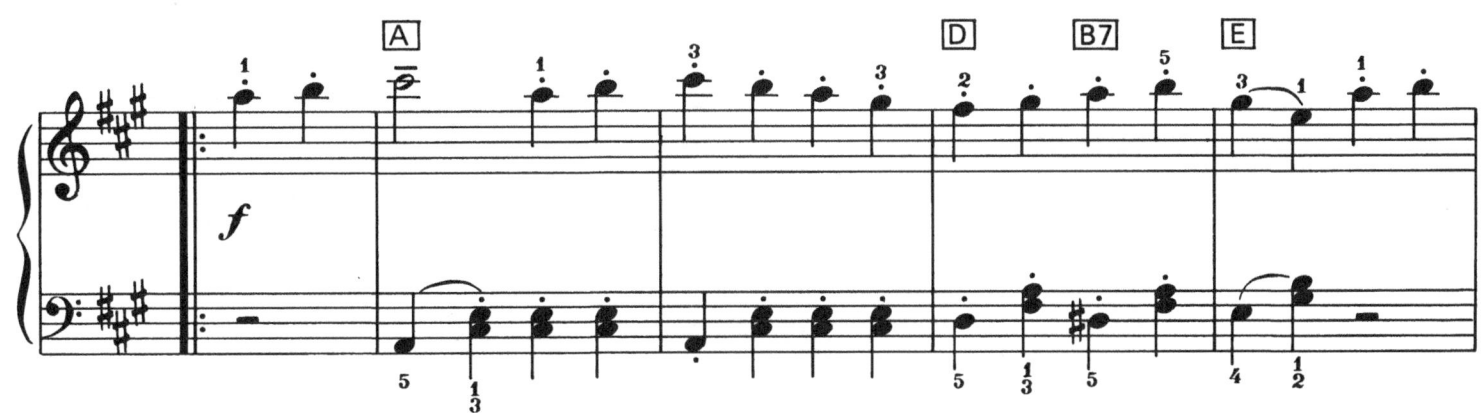
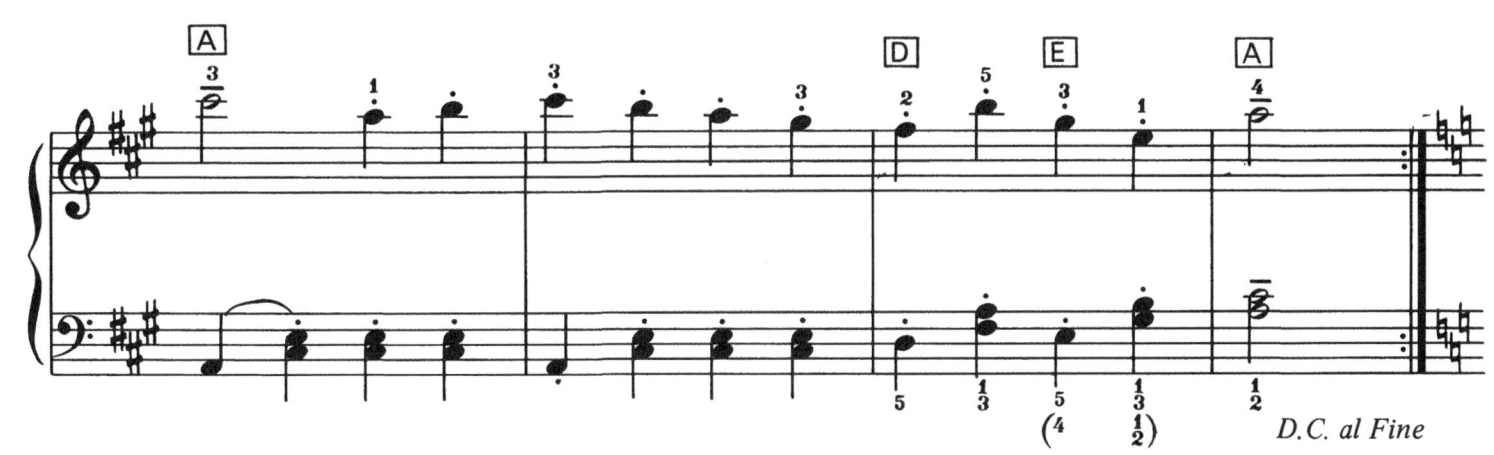

Mazurka
op. 37

Hans-Günter Heumann

*) Anmerkung für den Lehrer:
Kurze Vorschlagsnote ad libitum.

*) Notes for the teacher:
Short grace note ad lib.

© Copyright MCMLXXXVI by Bosworth & Co.

Alle Rechte vorbehalten
Alle rights reserved

Träumerei
Dreaming
aus den "Kinderszenen", op. 15

Robert Schumann (1810-1856)
Arr.: Hans-Günter Heumann